A Pocket
Christian Catechism

A Pocket
Christian Catechism

Keeping the Faith in the
Challenges of the 21st Century

Charles R. Ringma

Foreword by Alex Fogleman

RESOURCE *Publications* · Eugene, Oregon

Contents

Foreword

Many pastors, scholars, and pundits have opined the gradual—
and sometimes not so gradual—decline of biblical literacy over
the past several decades. Much handwringing ensues, but little
in the way of practical suggestions. Rather than lamenting this
murky state of affairs, Charles Ringma has given us this pocket
catechism as a small beacon of light to help us find our way out of
the fog. It's a deceptively brilliant work of theological instruction,
one that teaches more by showing than telling, by allowing us to
"make these words our own."

Ringma styles this book within the time-tested genre of
catechism, though with several distinctive twists. For one, it's not
written in the question-and-answer format but rather provides
a thoughtfully curated selection of passages from Scripture and
the Christian tradition that can be easily committed to memory.
This is especially needed for those of us who live in a culture
that thinks of memory as something that can be downloaded or
uploaded, but rarely ever "in-loaded" in the heart. This is a neces-
sary and welcome addition.

For another, this pocket catechism contains not only the important standards of the classic catechisms—the Apostles' Creed
and the Lord's Prayer—but also a host of texts from Scripture,
hymnody, liturgy, Christian history, and contemporary theology.
It is, in short, a carefully selected treasure trove from the entirety
of the Christian tradition—past and present, East and West.

Finally, interwoven between these treasures for the memory
are Ringma's own words of theological wisdom, distilled through
many years of teaching and pastoral experience in the church and
the mission field. Ringma's guidance here is subtle but profound,

and these words will offer Christian disciples new and old much-needed light for the journey towards Christian faithfulness.

Alex Fogleman, Assistant Research Professor of Theology at Baylor University, USA, and Director of the Catechesis Institute

Preface

Throughout the church's long history and particularly at various crucial times, Christians have attempted to summarize their faith as a guide for faith-formation and to highlight certain distinctives.

Today, many of these summaries as creeds and catechisms exist, but few play a role in the contemporary church. The Apostle's Creed is an important exception.

That this is so, should not surprise us. Present-day faith-communities display little sense of history and are not good at the formation of persons into the life of faith.

Moreover, the relativism of our post-modern world has left many Christians with little ground under their feet regarding faith and its practices.

Here then is a small attempt to orchestrate from the Scriptures and the creeds and catechisms of the church the central themes of the Christian faith for a life of love, worship, prayer, witness, and service.

The idea of this pocket catechism is to have it with you and to read it often. In it lies the hope that it will provide "ground" under our feet as we seek to be God's faithful people in Christ through the Holy Spirit in a time where dark clouds are gathering on the horizons of our lives and societies.

The climate crisis, pandemics, our surveillance societies, the dream and threat of artificial intelligence, job insecurities, scepticism about our major institutions, and major political shifts in our global world, all suggest that our present difficulties may well increase. And who knows what lies beyond the horizon.

In times of uncertainty the only constructive way to live is to face reality, dig wells of spiritual sustenance, remain hopeful in the God who journeys with us, and find ways to be a blessing to others.

God's gift of life-giving water may well sustain our spiritual practices and all that we seek to be and do in the journey of faith. This pocket catechism may well be one's daily bread and drink.

Charles Ringma,
Brisbane, Australia,
2023.

1

"Pray in the Spirit

at all times in every prayer and supplication.

To that end keep alert

and always persevere in supplication for all the saints."[1]

1. Ephesians 6:18, NRSV.

2
The Lord's Prayer

"Our Father in heaven,

hallowed be your name.

Your kingdom come.

Your will be done

on earth as it is in heaven.

Give us this day our daily bread.

And forgive us our debts,

as we have also forgiven our debtors.

And do not bring us to the time of trial

but rescue us from the evil one."[2]

Amen.

2. Matthew 6:9–13, NRSV.

3

"He has made everything beautiful

in its time.

Also, he has put eternity into

man's heart,

yet so that he cannot find out

what God has done

from the beginning to the end."[3]

---

3. Ecclesiastes 3:11, ESV.

4
The Great Longing

Humans are made in the image and likeness of God the creator. Thus, all of humanity is marked by the pristine goodness of God.

This profound connection means that God is towards us and calls us to relate to this Winsome Lover. Thus, within each of us lies the power of the invitation to the worship and love of God.

Sadly, this invitation is at times ignored or suppressed. But it always re-emerges in some form or other, though not necessarily in a God-ward direction.

Our great longing so easily gets diverted into self-love or other forms of idolatry, and so we create our own gods who divert us from the Winsome Lover. It is, therefore, true, that this great longing leaves us ever looking but not finding.

But there is good news. God the creator is also God the redeemer. God seeks us out. God woes us. God calls us. God's Spirit is the enabling Spirit who seeks to bring us on the journey homeward.

Thus, the great longing becomes the journey of faith in an encounter with the seeking God, who has drawn so hauntingly close in the incarnation of his Son, Jesus of Nazareth, who has appeared as the icon of the true humanity and the saviour of the world.

The great longing is to become the great embrace—caught up by faith in the grace and mercy of God. This marks our true homecoming.

Marked by the goodness of God—we all have a magnificent beginning! But so much of this goodness has been stillborn, since we have gone our own way. What folly! And so, we need to be saved from ourselves.

And this is what God, who goes the second mile, has provided. Christ the Saviour can refocus the great longing and make it fruitful unto life eternal.

"Therefore, since we are justified by faith, we have peace with God through our Lord Jesus Christ."[4] "So if anyone is in Christ, there is a new creation."[5]

4. Romans 5:1 NRSV.
5. 2 Corinthians 5:17, NRSV.

5

"God our Father

whose Son, the light unfailing,

has come from heaven to deliver the world

from the darkness of ignorance:

let these holy mysteries open the eyes of our understanding

that we may know the way of life,

and walk in it without stumbling

through Jesus Christ our Lord."[6]

---

6. *Common Worship*, 421.

6
The Apostles' Creed

"I believe in God, the Father almighty, creator of heaven and earth;

and in Jesus Christ, God's only Son, our Lord,

who was conceived by the Holy Spirit, born of the virgin Mary,

suffered under Pontius Pilate, was crucified, died and was buried.

He descended to the dead,

on the third day he rose again,

he ascended to heaven, he is seated at the right hand of the Father,

and he will come to judge the living and the dead.

I believe in the Holy Spirit, the holy catholic church,

the communion of saints,

the forgiveness of sins, the resurrection of the body,

and the life everlasting."[7]

7. *Celebrating Common Prayer,* 247–48.

7

"*Question*: What is your comfort in life and death?

Answer: That I, with body and soul, both in life and death,

am not my own, but belong to my faithful Saviour Jesus Christ,

who with his precious blood has fully satisfied for all my sins,

and delivered me from all the power of the devil. . .[and who]

by the Holy Spirit assures me of eternal life,

and makes me heartily willing and ready,

henceforth, to live unto him."[8]

8. "The Heidelberg Catechism," in *Psalter Hymnal,* 22.

8
The Grand Redemption

God's story is a grand story. And its sweep is magnificent and far-reaching from creational beginnings to the grand finale of new heavens and a new earth in the final purposes of God.

This grand story is marked by drama and passion. It is a story of the beauty of creation in the purposes of God. Its undoing is through human wilful disobedience and the human search for self-fulfilment and autonomy. And its recapitulation is through God's passion to restore and heal a wounded humanity.

There is no limit to the grand sweep of this narrative.

This story is not simply about the healing of the soul or the welcome to heaven. It is about that, but, o, so much more! For God's grand redemption is about personal healing, social well-being, human flourishing in the shalom of God, the passion for justice and care for the poor, and the healing of the nations in God's final future.

This sweeping story in the biblical narratives is told with honesty and persuasiveness. Its honesty lies in the litany of human stupidity in not following God's ways. Its persuasiveness lies in the pursuit by this "hound of heaven" through the brooding Spirit to bring humanity into all the goodness that God has already provided in Christ.

St. Paul exclaims: "that God was reconciling the world to himself in Christ" and that when "anyone is in Christ, he [she] is a new creation; the old has gone, the new has come!"[9]

9. 2 Corinthians 5:19, 17, NIV.

9

God's redemption offers a new start. And it offers a new way of being and living. The shape of this newness has to do with the life and way of Christ growing in us through the generative work of the Holy Spirit.

Through a common life with Christ, the faith-community is sustained through the Spirit as a worshipping, fellowshipping and serving community. It exists for the glory of God and to serve the human community for its well-being and redemption.

9
A Franciscan Prayer

"Thus,

inwardly cleansed,

interiorly enlightened,

and inflamed by the fire of the Holy Spirit,

may we be able to follow

in the footsteps of your beloved Son,

our Lord Jesus Christ."[10]

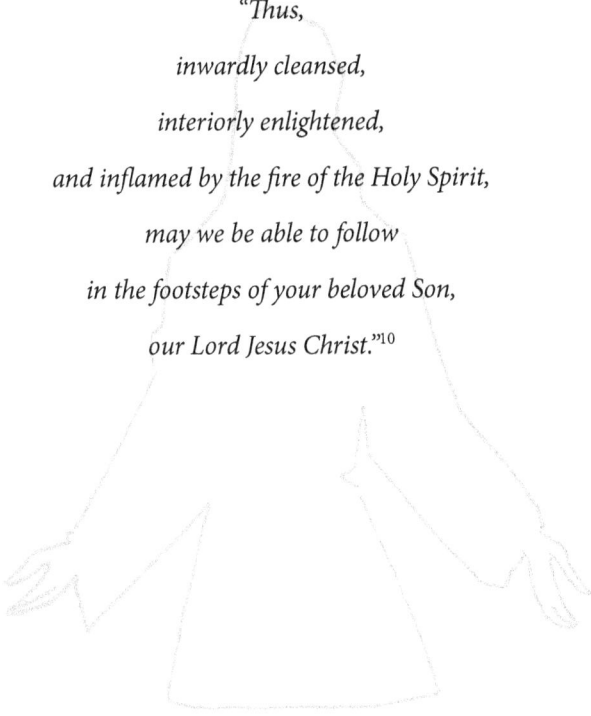

10. *Francis and Clare: The Complete Works,* 61.

10
The Beatitudes

"You're blessed when you're at the end of your rope.

> With less of you
> there is more of God and his rule.

You're blessed when you feel you've lost what is most dear to you.
Only then can you be embraced by the One most dear to you.

You're blessed when you're content with just who you are—no
more, no less. That's the moment you find yourselves proud own-
ers of everything that can't be bought.

You're blessed when you've worked up a good appetite for God.
He's food and drink in the best meal you'll ever eat.

You're blessed when you get your inside world—your mind and
your heart—put right. Then you can see God in the outside
world.

You're blessed when you can show people how to cooperate
instead of compete or fight. That's when you discover who you
really are, and your place in God's family.

You're blessed when your commitment to God provokes persecution. The persecution drives you even deeper into God's
kingdom."[11]

---

11. *The Message*, 1750–51.

11

"The new birth happens in human beings through the word of truth.

All who hear the gospel, and who, through the cooperation of the Holy Spirit, believe in Christ Jesus the only son of the living God, who is our Lord and Savior, are born of God, enlightened and taught by the Holy Spirit.

We ought not to begin or conclude anything other than what Christ has taught us and for which he was the example.

He is the beginning and end of all things. He is the leader of our faith and we look to him. He is the true light which has come into the world and we are his disciples."[12]

---

12. Dirk Philips, "Concerning the New Birth and the New Creature" (1556) in *Early Anabaptist Spirituality*, 202, 207.

12
The Beauty of Jesus, the Christ

The gospels are the lilting testimonies concerning the story of Jesus. They speak of his love for the Father, and his healing work of restoration for broken people.

The gospels highlight the incarnation, life, death, and resurrection of Jesus within the frame that Christ, as Lord and Saviour, was God come amongst us to provide the way of salvation and renewal for all humanity.

The epistles in appropriating the story of Jesus for the faith-communities in the Roman world, speak of Jesus in grand terms. He was with the Father from before time. He is the direct image of the Father. He is God Immanuel. He is the icon of the new humanity. He is the Lord of history and the one who holds all things together.

Combining the gospel and epistle reflections on Jesus, we can celebrate that Jesus came to save us from our sins and heal us from our woundedness, and that he came to dwell in us by the presence of the Holy Spirit. Thus, the story of Jesus is not simply information *about* him, but is the story of Christ as a *living and formative presence* in those who have turned to him in faith.

This dynamic issues in a life of becoming more and more like Christ. And this expresses itself in a myriad of ways—forming faith-communities, a life of obedience to the gospel, being led by Spirit, praying for the world, serving our neighbours, raising a prophetic voice against all forms of exploitation, working for a just peace in our world, and engaging in care for planet earth.

The story of Jesus as the great restorer, is a story of beauty and well-being. It is about forgiveness, welcome, healing, and celebration. Jesus is God's banquet table for humanity.

And the faith-community is called to sit at God's table and to be nourished and to bring friends and the poor to partake as well. What a celebration!

Thus, the beauty and goodness of Jesus is not frozen in the past as some miraculous story. It is also a present story. The followers of Jesus are called to the *imitatio Christi* and the faith-communities are called to be a second incarnation, living and proclaiming to beauty of the One in whom is life in all its fulness.

And so, the story continues. God's presence is amongst us. The Spirit makes us alive in Christ and leads the community to be an instrument of God's peace.

13

"*Cheap grace is the preaching of forgiveness without requiring repentance, baptism without church discipline, communion without confession. . .[it] is grace without discipleship, grace without the cross, grace without Jesus Christ, living and incarnate.*

Grace. . .is costly because it cost a man his life, and it is grace because it gives a man [woman] the only true life."[13]

---

13. Dietrich Bonhoeffer, *The Cost of Discipleship*, 36, 37.

14
The Barmen Declaration (1934)

"We pledge ourselves to the following evangelical truths. . .Jesus Christ, as he is testified to us in Holy Scripture, is the one Word of God, whom we are to hear, whom we are to obey in life and in death.

We repudiate the false teaching that the church can and must recognize yet other happenings and powers, images, and truths as divine revelation alongside this one Word of God. . .[and] that there are areas of our life in which we belong not to Jesus Christ, but to another lord. . .[and] that the church can turn over the form of her message and ordinances at will or according to some dominant ideological and political convictions. . .

The commission of the church, in which her freedom is founded, consists in this: in place of Christ and thus in the service of his own word and work, to extend through word and sacrament the message of the free grace of God to all people."[14]

The Augsburg Confession

"[The church] is the assembly of all believers among who the Gospel is preached in its purity and the holy sacraments are administered according to the Gospel."[15]

---

14. *Creeds of the Churches*, 518–22.

15. The Lutheran "Augsburg Confession" (1530) in *Creeds of the Churches*, 70.

The Second Helvetic Confession

"[The church] is a company of the faithful called and gathered out of the world; a communion. . .of all saints. . .who truly know and rightly worship and serve the true God, in Jesus Christ the Saviour, by the word and the Holy Spirit, and who by faith are partakers of all those good graces which are freely offered through Christ."[16]

16. The Reformed "Second Helvetic Confession" (1566) in *Creeds of the Churches*, 141.

15

"We believe in. . .a visible church of God, consisting of those. . .who. . .have truly repented, and rightly believed; who are rightly baptized, united with God in heaven, and incorporated into the communion of the saints on earth."[17]

"The mystery of the holy church is already brought to light in the manner of its foundation. For the Lord Jesus inaugurated his church by preaching the good news of the coming kingdom of God. . .When Jesus, having died on the cross for humanity, rose again from the dead, he appeared as Lord. . .and he poured out on his disciples the Spirit promised by the Father. . .[T]he church, equipped with the gifts of its founder and faithfully observing his precepts of charity. . .receives the mission of proclaiming and establishing among all peoples the kingdom of Christ and of God."[18]

"The purpose of God. . .is to gather the whole of creation under the Lordship of Christ Jesus, in whom, by the power of the Holy Spirit, all are brought into communion with God. . .The church is the foretaste of this communion with God and with one another. The grace of our Lord Jesus Christ, the love of God, and the communion of the Holy Spirit enable the one church to live as a sign of the reign of God. . .The purpose of the church is to unite people with Christ in the power of the Spirit, to manifest communion in prayer and action and thus to point to the fullness of communion with God, humanity, and the whole creation in the glory of the kingdom."[19]

---

17. The Anabaptist "Dordrecht Confession" (1632) in *Creeds of the Churches*, 299.

18. Roman Catholic "Lumen Gentium" (1964) in *Vatican Council II*, 4.

19. World Council of Churches "The Unity of the Church as Koinonia: Gift and Calling" (1991) in *The Ecumenical Movement*, 124.

16
The Nature and Calling of the Faith-Community

The church—the faith-community—is both a religious institution and the body of Christ. The latter is its fundamental nature.

This community consists of those who are "bound" to Christ by faith through the life-giving Spirit and who share common practices of worship, attending to the Word, participating in the sacraments, sharing life together (*koinonia*), and serving one another and the wider community (*diakonia*).

Thus, this faith-community is oriented towards God, towards each other, and towards the wider world. In its orientation towards God, the formative processes have to do with worship, prayer, and obedience, Practices in relation to each other have to do with church participation, growing in community, and in the practices of hospitality and generosity. And the community's orientation towards the world has to do with service and witness.

A particular local church needs to see itself as part of the wider church and of global Christianity. Moreover, it should also see itself as part of the church throughout the ages and should learn from the church's long two-thousand-year journey in history. It should see itself as part of the faithful who have died in faith and who await, with us, God's final future.

The faith-community is one body in Christ with its members exercising differing gifts and abilities. All of these should be welcomed so that the community may grow in Christlikeness, discipleship, and service.

This community is to be a second "incarnation" in that it seeks to be a living embodiment of the way of Christ. In this way, it seeks to be both a witness and sign to the kingdom of God in

Christ. It's calling is to glorify God and to be servant of the coming reign of God.

This means that this community must always live, in faith and repentance, in prayer and good works, and in humility and service, in order to be this sign of the way of Christ.

The faith-community is a pilgrim community. It is on the way—it has not arrived. It is a community of forgiveness—not one in the community is perfect. It is a prophetic community resisting the powers of this age. And it is a welcoming community—come and see!

17

"In the evening, and the morning, and at noon,
we praise and bless you,

we pray to you in thanksgiving and supplication.

Father of all, may our prayers be set before you like incense

and may our hearts not yield

to the words of the wicked.

Deliver us from all who seek to take possession of our souls.

For our eyes are fixed, on you, O Lord,

our refuge is in you

and you are our hope.

Do not abandon us, O Lord our God.

For to you belong all glory, honor, and worship,

Father, Son, and Holy Spirit,

now and forever, to the ages of ages. Amen."

Prayer of the Eastern Orthodox Church[20]

20. *The Doubleday Prayer Collection*, 283.

18
The Grand Old Testament Covenant

"So now, O Israel, what does the Lord your God require of you?

Only to fear the Lord your God, to walk in all his ways, to love him,

to serve the Lord your God with all your heart

and with all your soul,

and to keep the commandments of the Lord your God

and his decrees

that I am commanding you today, for your own well-being.

Although heaven and the heaven of heavens belong

to the Lord your God,

the earth with all that is in it,

yet the Lord set his heart in love on your ancestors alone

and chose you,

their descendants after them

out of all the peoples, as it is today.

Circumcise, then, the foreskin of your heart. . .

For the Lord your God is. . .mighty and

awesome, who is not partial and takes no bribe, who executes

justice for the orphan

and the widow, and who loves strangers. . .

You shall also love the stranger, for you were strangers
in the land of Egypt.

You shall fear the Lord your God; him alone you shall worship;

to him you shall hold

fast. . .He is your praise; he is your God."[21]

21. Deuteronomy 10:12–21, NRSV.

19

"To believe in the Holy Spirit

is to profess that the Holy Spirit is one of the

persons of the Holy Trinity,

consubstantial with the Father and the Son."[22]

"The Holy Spirit is at work with the Father and the Son

from the beginning

to the completion of the plan of our salvation."[23]

"What the soul is to the human body,

the Holy Spirit is to the Body of Christ, which is the Church."[24]

"The Holy Spirit

makes the Church 'the temple of the living God.'"[25]

"Christ. . .pours out the Holy Spirit

among his members

22. *Catechism of the Catholic Church,* 169.
23. *Catechism,* 170.
24. *Catechism,* 196.
25. *Catechism,* 196.

to nourish, heal. . .to give them life, [and] send them

to bear witness."[26]

"The Spirit prepares men [women] and goes out to them

with his grace,

in order to draw them to Christ."[27]

"The Holy Spirit, the artisan of God's works,

is the master of prayer."[28]

26. *Catechism,* 182.
27. *Catechism,* 181.
28. *Catechism,* 182.

20
The Enabling and Renewing Holy Spirit

The New Testament frequently speaks of the blessing of the Father, the Son, and the Holy Spirit, and the confessions of the church testify that God is Father, Son, and Holy Spirit, and that each of the "persons" of the Trinity are involved with and in each other's work. The Trinity is like a sacred communal dance.

While much of the New Testament focusses on the person and work of Christ, the Holy Spirit is promised as a special presence in and with the followers of Jesus and in the life of the church. The Spirit also works beyond the church renewing the face of the earth, beautifying humanity, and bringing Christ home to all who seek him.

The Spirit is the greatest gift we can receive because the Spirit births us into Christ, sustains us in our spiritual journey, and scatters wonderful gifts on the faith-community, including wisdom, healing, discernment, prophecy, caring, and planning, among other gifts.

The Spirit is the creative and empowering spirit. Creativity and beauty are inspired by the Spirit. Those seeking to serve and to bring about change are empowered by Spirit.

But the Spirit is not simply the serving Spirit. The Spirit partakes of the Lordship of Christ and thus works sovereignly in people's lives, the church, and the world. Thus, the Spirit will do what the Spirit wishes to do. As such, the Spirit is the troubling Spirit, the challenging Spirit, and the renewing Spirit.

Whenever people become repentant, the Spirit is at work. Wherever the faith-community seeks to live in greater fidelity to the gospel, the Spirit is present. Whenever people turn in faith to embrace Christ, the Spirit is drawing them into the life of Christ.

And when human creativity spills into oratorios, chamber music, art, community change, and political agitation, the brooding Spirit is at work.

The challenge to each of us is to be open to the work of the Spirit, the gentle presence with us. But at the same time, we need the Spirit to nudge us, turn us around, and to lead us on.

Our daily prayer: Come, Holy Spirit, Come!

21

"If the task of prophecy is to empower people to engage in history,
then it means evoking cries that expect answers,
learning to address them where they will be taken seriously,
and ceasing to look to the numbed and dull empire
that never intended to answer in the first place."[29]

"The prophet engages in a futuring fantasy.
The prophet does not ask if the vision can be implemented. . .
***imagination** must come before the **implementation**."*[30]

"The prophet. . .has only the hope
*that the **ache** of God could penetrate the **numbness** of history.*
He engages not in scare or threat
but only in a yearning that grows with and out of pain."[31]

"It is the task of prophetic imagination. . .
to bring people to engage the promise of newness
that is at work in our history with God."[32]

29. Brueggemann, *The Prophetic Imagination*, 13.
30. *The Prophetic Imagination*, 40.
31. *The Prophetic Imagination*, 55.
32. *The Prophetic Imagination*, 59–60.

22
The Prophetic Imagination

"The spirit of the Lord Yahweh has been given me,

for Yahweh has anointed me.

He has sent me to bring good news to the poor,

to bind up hearts that are broken;

to proclaim liberty to captives,

freedom to those in prison;

to proclaim a year of favour from Yahweh,

a day of vengeance for our God,

to comfort all those who mourn

and to give them for ashes a garland;

for mourning robe the oil of gladness,

for despondency, praise.

They are to be called terebinths of integrity,

planted by Yahweh to glorify him.

They will rebuild the ancient ruins,

they will raise what has long lain waste,

they will restore the ruined cities,

all that has lain waste for ages past."[33]

33. Isaiah 61:1–13, The Jerusalem Bible.

23

"We cannot always offer up uniform prayers.

We pray one way when we are invigorated

by spiritual achievements

and another way when we are cast down by the burden of attacks."

John Cassian (c.360–435)[34]

"The fruit and purpose of our prayers. . .is that we will be

united with our Lord and like him in all things."

Julian of Norwich (c.1342–1413)[35]

"Where there is inner peace and meditation,

there is neither anxiousness nor dissipation."

St. Francis of Assisi (1181–1226)[36]

"What I say is that someone who lives the

contemplative life may—indeed, must—

be absolutely free from outward works when engaged

34. "The Conferences of John Cassian," in Ringma & Alexander, eds. *Of Martyrs, Monks, and Mystics,* 33.

35. "Revelations of Divine Love Shewed to a Devout Ankress," in *Of Martyrs, Monks, and Mystics,* 87.

36. "The Admonitions of St. Francis," in *Of Martyrs, Monks, and Mystics,* 199.

in the act of contemplation,

but afterwards, his or her duty lies in outward service."

Meister Eckhart (c.1260–327)[37]

"For the honour of fasting consists not in abstinence from food,

but in withdrawing

from sinful practices. . .let not the mouth only fast,

but also the eye, and the ear,

and the feet, and the hands."

St. John Chrysostom (c.347–407)[38]

37. "The Best of Meister Eckhart," in *Of Martyrs, Monks, and Mystics*, 60.
38. "Homilies," in *Of Martyrs, Monks, and Mystics*, 292.

24
Formation in Spiritual Practices

The Christian life is formed and shaped in a variety of ways. These include the common practices of the faith-community—worship, Word, sacrament, fellowship, and service—and the personal practices of each follower of Jesus. Here we will focus on these personal practices.

Traditionally personal practices have included prayer, meditation, contemplation, fasting, and almsgiving or gifts of generosity. But they may also include the practices of creativity and hospitality and other forms of service. And obviously, we are shaped by family, education, and work.

The core idea in relation to these practices is not that they add *value* to our spiritual lives and in our relation to God. Our life with and for God is marked by grace. It is not a mercantile endeavour.

So, what then is the purpose of these spiritual practices? There are many!

First, they are birthed, sustained, and flourish in our lives due the life-giving Spirit. Thus, spiritual practices are signs that God is at work in us.

Second, spiritual practices reflect our most basic values. To live with the sense that we need God, need to pray, and participate in other practices, shows that we believe that mere self-sufficiency is not the way we wish to live.

Third, we believe that spiritual practices, such as prayer and radical hospitality, among others, reflect the gospel. Thus, these practices incarnate what we believe the Christian life is all about. They are an embodied gospel.

Fourth, spiritual practices are key to a life of witness and service. Prayer should precede and accompany all that we seek to do. To contemplate the gospel, the society, and our own lives, suggests that we seek to come at all things with a reflective posture. We seek to gain insight and inspiration before we engage in the fray of life.

But possibly the most important practice is an attentive engagement with Scripture through both scholarly and meditative reading so that we become immersed in its wisdom and seek to live that with fidelity.

Hearing and obeying are core dynamics in the Christian life. And we read Scripture to be attentive to God's voice and are willing to be corrected by its instructions. Blessed are those who hear the word of God and do it!

25

"O merciful Father

who gave your Son, Jesus Christ, to be the good shepherd,

and in his love for us

to lay down his life and rise again:

keep us ever under his protection,

and give us grace to follow in his steps;

through Jesus Christ our Lord."[39]

"God of our pilgrimage,

who has willed that the gate of mercy

should stand open for those who trust in you:

look upon us with your favour

that we, following in the path of your will,

may never wander from the way of life;

through Jesus Christ our Lord."[40]

39. *Common Worship,* 474.
40. *Common Worship,* 486.

26
The Lord is My Shepherd (Psalm 23)

"The Lord is my shepherd;

therefore can I lack nothing.

He makes me lie down in green pastures

and leads me beside still waters.

He shall refresh my soul

and guide me in the paths of righteousness

for his name's sake.

Though I walk through the valley of the shadow of death,

I will fear no evil;

for you are with me;

your rod and your staff, they comfort me.

You spread a table before me

in the presence of those who trouble me;

you have anointed my head with oil

and my cup shall be full.

Surely goodness and loving mercy shall follow me

all the days of my life,

and I will dwell in the house of the Lord forever."[41]

41. *Common Worship*, 617.

27

"If you confess with your mouth that Jesus Christ is Lord

and believe in your heart

that God raised him from the dead, you will be saved."[42]

"For us there is one God, the Father

from whom are all things and for whom we exist,

and one Lord, Jesus Christ,

through whom are all things and through whom we exist."[43]

"Christ died for our sins in accordance with the Scriptures,

that he was buried, and that he was raised on the third day."[44]

"He [Christ] was manifested in the flesh,

vindicated by the Spirit, seen by angels,

proclaimed among the nations, believed on in the world,

taken up in glory."[45]

42. Romans 10:9–10, ESV.
43. 1 Corinthians 8:6, ESV.
44. 1 Corinthians 15:3–4, ESV.
45. 1 Timothy 3:16, ESV.

"For to this you have been called, because Christ
also suffered for you, leaving you an
example, so that you might follow in his steps.
He committed no sin, neither was
deceit found in his mouth. When he was reviled,
he did not revile in return; when he
suffered, he did not threaten, but continued
entrusting himself to him who judges
justly."[46]

46. 1 Peter 2:21–23, ESV.

28
Faith Formation in Early Christianity

The earliest followers of Jesus sought to proclaim Jesus as Saviour and Lord, formed faith-communities in which to sustain and grow in the faith, and formulated key sayings that were partial summaries of what they believed. But these summaries, such as those on the opposite page, also expressed the way the early believers lived.

These Christians also gave the faith-communities a certain organisational shape and gave a lot of attention to how seekers might be formed into the faith and how they might become part of its life together.

The following steps in faith formation can be identified:

- Persons underwent a long catechumenate—instruction in the faith. Often this was over a period of several years. Hippolytus (c.170–235) suggests, three years. But this may be shortened if a person is "keen and perseveres well in the matter."[47]

- In preparation for baptism, they were asked if they had "lived uprightly," and had performed the "good works" of faith.[48]

- A further step involved the bishop praying prayers of exorcism over baptismal candidates: "he shall exorcize them of every foreign spirit and they shall flee away from them."[49]

- The candidate is baptized in water confessing that he believes "in God the Father Almighty," is dipped again in

47. Hippolytus, *On the Apostolic Tradition*, 103.
48. *On the Apostolic Tradition*, 105–6.
49. *On the Apostolic Tradition*, 106.

water confessing faith "in Christ Jesus, the son of God," and on confessing belief "in the Holy Spirit" is "baptized a third time."[50]

- The candidate is then anointed with oil and the following prayer is said: "I anoint you with the holy oil in God the Father Almighty and Jesus Christ and the Holy Spirit."[51]

The sharing of the Eucharistic bread was followed by the instruction: "hurry to do good works, to please God and to live properly, being devoted to the church putting into action what he [she] has learnt and progressing in piety."[52]

50. *On the Apostolic Tradition*, 111–12.
51. *On the Apostolic Tradition*, 112.
52. *On the Apostolic Tradition*, 113.

29

"Almighty God, unto whom

all hearts are open, all desires known,

and from whom no secrets are hid:

cleanse the thoughts of our hearts by the inspiration

of your Holy Spirit,

that we may perfectly love you,

and worthily magnify your holy name;

through Christ our Lord. Amen."[53]

"O God our defender,

storms rage about us and cause us to be afraid.

Rescue your people from despair. . .

and preserve us from all unbelief;

through your Son, Jesus Christ our Lord."[54]

"Almighty God,

you have made us for yourself,

and our hearts are restless until they find their rest in you.

May we find peace in your service,

---

53. *The Book of Alternative Services*, 230.
54. *The Book of Alternative Services*, 363.

and in the world to come, see you face to face;

through Jesus Christ our Lord,

who lives and reigns with you and the Holy Spirit,

one God, now and for ever."[55]

55. *The Book of Alternative Services*, 367.

30
Be Thou My Vision

"Be thou my vision, O Lord of my heart,
naught be all else to me, save that thou art—
thou my best thought by day or by night,
waking or sleeping, thy presence my light.

Be thou my wisdom, be thou my true word;
I ever with thee, thou with me, Lord;
thou my great Father, I thy true son;
thou in me dwelling, and I with thee one.

Be thou my battle-shield, my sword for the fight,
be thou my dignity, thou my delight;
thou my soul's shelter, thou my high tower:
raise thou me heaven-ward, O power of my power.

Riches I heed not, nor man's empty praise,
thou my inheritance, now and always:
thou and thou only, first in my heart,
high king of heaven, my treasure thou art.

High King of heaven, after victory won,

May I reach heaven's joys, O bright heaven's Sun;

heart of my own heart, whatever befall,

still be my vision, O ruler of all."[56]

---

56. Irish hymn c. 8th century, *The Australian Hymn Book,* 572.

3 1

"Therefore, since we are justified by faith, we have peace with God through our Lord Jesus Christ through whom we have obtained access to this grace in which we stand; and we boast in our hope of sharing the glory of God. . .but we also boast in our sufferings, knowing that suffering produces endurance, and endurance produces character, and character produces hope, and hope does not disappoint us, because God's love has been poured into our hearts through the Holy Spirit that has been given to us."[57]

"Jesus answered, 'Those who are well have no need of a physician, but those who are sick; I have come to call not the righteous but sinners to repentance.'"[58]

"Have mercy on me, O God, according to your steadfast love; according to your abundant mercy blot out my transgressions. Wash me thoroughly from my iniquity, and cleanse me from my sin. . .Create in me a clean heart, O God, and put a new and right spirit within me."[59]

57. Romans 5:1–5, NRSV.
58. Luke 5:31–32, NRSV.
59. Psalm 51:1–2, 10, NRSV.

32
Faith, Repentance, and Conversion

There are many dimensions to the life of faith. It is like a tapestry with many designs and colours. We should be careful that we don't reduce the spiritual journey to single themes.

The heart of the good news is that God is the one who seeks us out and calls us into relationship—a relationship of embrace, healing, and forgiveness. What we are to do is to respond to God's leading, and even in our doing God helps us.

Our most basic response is to accept what God offers us in his Word and by his Spirit.

Our response to what God offers in Christ, is a faith response. In this response we not only believe but also trust, and more profoundly, we commit ourselves to God and God's way for us. Thus, faith involves a living relationship and a whole of life endeavour. In other words, we live the whole of our life by faith in the God who has embraced us in Christ.

But God's call is not only a call to come to God's provision in Christ, but is also a call to leave our own ways. And since these ways are self-orchestrated and not God-centred, we need to walk the pathways of repentance.

The beginnings of repentance lie in the heart-cry: God be merciful to me a sinner! But the call to repentance remains a theme in the Christian life, for we fall short in loving God "with all your heart, and with all your soul, and with all your mind, and with all your strength."[60] And we have long way to go in living the call "to put away your former way of life, your old self. . .and to be renewed in the spirit of your minds, and to clothe yourselves

60. Mark 12:30, NRSV.

46

with the new self, created according to the likeness of God in true righteousness and holiness."[61]

All of this means that conversion—this turning to God and away from our own self-determinations—is to be our daily bread. The conversion of the heart also involves a conversion from the "fallen powers"—the ideologies and psychopathologies of our culture—in order to live in God's way and to be a prophetic and healing presence in our world.

---

61. Ephesians 4:22–23, NRSV.

33

"We believe in the Holy Spirit, which establishes the
holy catholic church.

We are the church: the people who believe the good news about
Jesus, who are baptized, and who share in the Lord's Supper.

Through these means of grace, the Spirit renews us
so that we may serve God in love.

All those who live in union with Christ, whether on earth
or with God in heaven, are saints.

Our communion with Christ makes us members one of another.

As by his death Christ removed our separation from God,
so by his Spirit Christ removes all that divides us from each other.

Breaking down every wall of hostility, the Spirit makes us,
who are many, one body in Christ.

God does not will to be God without us, but instead grants
to us creatures, eternal life.

Communion with Jesus is eternal life itself.

By the Holy Spirit, we are joined to Christ through faith,
and adopted as children, the sons and daughters of God.

Through Christ we are raised from death to new life.

For Christ we shall live to all eternity."[62]

62. *Belonging to God: Catechism Resources for Worship*, 20.

34
Come, Holy Spirit, Come!

If ever there was a prayer that needs to daily reside in our hearts it is: Come, Holy Spirit, Come!

We need the Spirit to renew the face of the earth. We need the Spirit to blow the winds of change and renewal.

We need the Spirit to bring the presence of Christ to us and to revitalize the faith-community.

We need the Spirit's fruits and gifts to make us into God's beautiful people.

We need the Spirit to move us to love the poor, to seek justice, and shalom for all.

Come, Holy Spirit, Come!

Prayer for the Spirit

"Pour into our hearts the sentiment of Your love,
become Yourself a flowing current for us.

For our own current does not carry us all the way to You.

Be rainfall upon our parchedness, be a river through our landscape,
that it might find in You a defining middle and a cause
of its increasing and bearing fruit.

And should Your water bring forth blossoms and fruit in us,
then let us not regard these as our own sproutings and produce,
for they stem from you.

And let us lay them up in advance with You, adding to the store
of invisible goods that You can dispose of as you wish.

They are fruits from your land, brought forth by You,
which are Yours to use for You or for us, or to reserve
for another who has nothing."[63]

---

63. Hans Urs von Balthasar, *Credo: Meditations on the Apostle's Creed*, 105.

35

"Baptism [in water] which follows preaching and believing, is not that which makes a person godly. It is a sign only, a covenant, a parable and memorial. . .of *true* baptism. [True baptism is where] God makes His own blessed and worthy through the bonds of the new birth and renewal of the Holy Spirit in faith. Whoever would be a disciple of the Lord must be baptized and made pure in the Holy Spirit and be united by the bonds of peace into one body."[64]

"Baptism is a sacrament of the New Testament, ordained by Jesus Christ. . .[for] admission. . .into the visible Church, but also [as]. . .a sign and seal of the covenant of grace, of. . .ingrafting into Christ, of regeneration, of remission of sins, and of. . .giving up unto God, through Jesus Christ, to walk in newness of life."[65]

"Through baptism I am adopted and welcomed into God's family. In the water of baptism I share in the dying and rising of Jesus, who washes away my sins. I am made one with him and with all who are joined to him in the church."[66]

"The baptized, by regeneration and the anointing of the Holy Spirit, are consecrated as a spiritual house and a holy priesthood, that through all their Christian activities they may offer spiritual

64. Hans Hut, "One the Mystery of Baptism" (1526) in *Early Anabaptist Spirituality,* 73, 74.

65. "Westminster Confession of Faith" (1646), in *Creeds of the Churches,* 224.

66. *Belonging to God,* 26.

sacrifices and proclaim the marvels of him who called them out of darkness into his wonderful light."[67]

"Administered in obedience to our Lord, baptism is a sign and seal of our common discipleship. Through baptism, Christians are brought into union with Christ, with each other and with the Church of every time and place. Our common baptism, which unites us to Christ in faith, is thus a basic bond of unity. . .When baptismal unity is realized in one holy, catholic, apostolic Church, a genuine Christian witness can be made to the healing and reconciling love of God."[68]

67. "Lumen Gentium," in *The Basic Sixteen Documents, Vatican Council II*, 14.

68. "WCC Commission on Faith and Order, Lima, 1982," in *The Ecumenical Movement*, 179.

36
Baptisms: Life-Giving Dimensions

Paul's letter to the Ephesians with its emphasis on unity speaks of baptism: "There is one body and one Spirit—just as you were called to the one hope that belongs to your call—one Lord, one faith, one baptism, one God and Father of all, who is over all and through all and in all."[69]

But this baptism is many-dimensional. The Anabaptist tradition speaks of three baptisms: the baptism of new birth into a faith relationship with Christ through the Holy Spirit; a water baptism into the faith-community expressing a commitment to formation, discipline, sharing, and service; and a baptism of "blood" in following the suffering Christ into the world.

The Pentecostal and Charismatic traditions emphasise two baptisms following conversion. The one is a baptism in the Spirit which empowers the believer in Christ for service and brings the charismatic gifts of the Spirit into expression. The other baptism is baptism in water, which may precede or follow Spirit baptism, and is a sign and seal of one's relation to Christ and one's participation in the faith-community.

The Roman Catholic and mainstream Protestant churches make infant baptism the foundational move of one's incorporation into Christ and into the church with its subsequent unfolding into one's confession of faith and one's mature participation of the faith-community.

These perspectives have divided the church for centuries. This reflection won't bring resolution, but here are some key texts—

69. Ephesians 4:4–6, ESV.

"All of us who have baptized into Christ were baptized into his death. . .[that] we. . .might walk in newness of life."[70]

"For in one Spirit we were all baptized into one body—Jews or Greeks, slaves or free—and all were made to drink of one Spirit."[71]

"John answered. . .I baptize you with water. . .He will baptize you with the Holy Spirit and fire."[72] And, "are you able to drink the cup that I drink, or be baptized with the baptism with which I am baptized"?[73]

All of this speaks of a powerful impact through water and the Spirit that marks us for life as a disciple of Christ and member of the community of faith.

70. Romans 6:3–4, ESV.
71. 1 Corinthians 12:13, ESV.
72. Luke 3:16, ESV.
73. Mark 10:38, ESV.

"Father, we plead with confidence his sacrifice made once for all on the cross; we remember his dying and rising in glory, and we rejoice that he intercedes for us at your right hand.

Pour out your Holy Spirit as we bring before you these gifts of your creation; may they be for us the body and blood of your dear Son.

As we eat and drink these holy things in your presence, form us into the likeness of Christ, and build us into a living temple to your glory."[74]

"In Christ, the new Adam, the perfect man, this eucharistic life was restored to man [woman]. For He Himself was the perfect Eucharist; He offered Himself in total obedience, love, and thanksgiving to God. . .And thus this offering to God of bread and wine, of the food we must eat to live, is our offering to Him of ourselves."[75]

"Eucharistic celebrations are for the sake of a eucharistic life in which we worship the Father, and, like Jesus, become through the Holy Spirit bread and wine for a hungry and thirsty world."[76]

"The words and acts of Jesus at the institution of the eucharist stand at the heart of the celebration; the eucharistic meal is the

74. *Common Worship*, 203.
75. Schmemann, *For the Life the World*, 34–35.
76. Cunningham & Egan, *Christian Spirituality*, 198.

sacrament of the body and blood of Christ, the sacrament of his real presence."[77]

"In the eucharist we not only commune with Jesus, but with his Kingdom project; we not only edify the church but anticipate the banquet of the Kingdom. Thus, the eucharist is inseparable from the fellowship of love and service."[78]

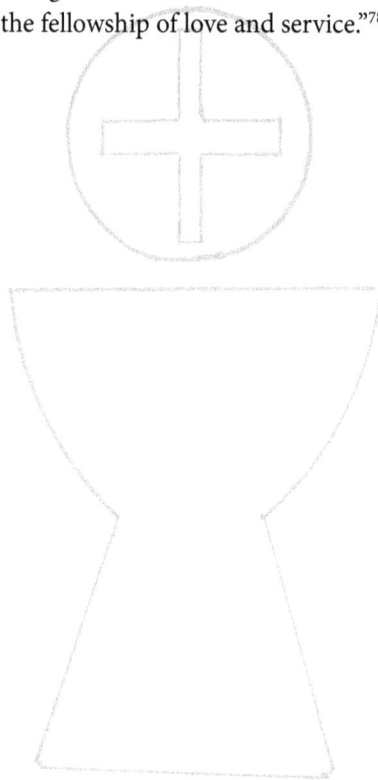

77. "WCC Commission on Faith and Order, Lima, 1982," in *The Ecumenical Movement*, 185.

78. Victor Codina, "Sacraments," in *Mysterium Liberationis*, 671.

38
Living the Eucharist

The life of faith nurtured in the faith-community—a community of the Word, worship, sacramental participation, fellowship, and service—is a life of joy, celebration, and receptivity.

The heartbeat of the Christian life is receiving the gifts of God. And one such beautiful gift is to receive the presence of Christ through the Spirit in the Eucharist. This gift reminds us of the generosity of God. It's a partaking of God's banquet table.

This great generosity reminds us that we are to live a eucharistic life—a life of generosity towards others, including the poor. It also reminds us that much-having is not the major theme of life, but grateful receiving and heartfelt generosity is the melody of the Christian life.

The New Testament has much to say about this wonderful celebration. Let these words shape our very life.

"And he took bread, gave thanks and broke it, and gave it to them, saying, 'This is my body given for you; do this in remembrance of me.' In the same way, after supper he took the cup, saying, 'This cup is the new covenant in my blood, which is poured out for you.'"[79]

"Then Jesus declared, 'I am the bread of life. He who comes to me will never go hungry, and he who believes in me will never be thirsty.'"[80]

"Is not the cup of thanksgiving for which we give thanks a participation in the blood of Christ? And is not the bread that we

79. Luke 22:19–20, NIV.
80. John 6:35, NIV.

break a participation in the body of Christ? Because there is one loaf, we, who are many, are one body, for we all partake of the one loaf."[81]

"But when you give a banquet, invite the poor, the crippled, the lame, the blind, and you will be blessed."[82]

"Then the angel showed me the river of the water of life, as clear as crystal, flowing from the throne of God. . .One each side of the river stood the tree of life. . .the leaves of the tree are for the healing of the nations."[83]

81. 1 Corinthians 10:16–17, NIV.
82. Luke 14:13, NIV.
83. Revelation 22: 1–2, NIV.

39

"Eternal God our Father,

you have accepted us as living members

of the Body of your Son, Jesus Christ our Lord,

and you have nourished us with the Sacrament

of his victorious life.

May we now be bread broken and given to the world,

may your love in us heal the wounds we have made,

may your words on our lips speak peace to all.

Send us with vision and strength to serve your Son

in the least of his brothers and sisters.

So will your name be praised and glorified,

now and in time to come,

until all be fulfilled in your Kingdom."[84]

84. Eucharistic Liturgy from the Independent Church of the Philippines in
From Shore to Shore, 13.

40
Eucharistic Liturgies from the Philippines and Sri Lanka

"Accept, O God, this sacrifice of thanksgiving and praise.

Quicken and awaken with your Spirit's power

this people, bread and cup,

that they truly all become,

in flesh and blood, the very 'Truth'[85] transformed by your mighty

power . . .

United now with the oppressed ones,

and in their struggle to birth the new age,

we declare freedom for all and a common weal

in partaking by your mighty power."[86]

85. The word in the text is "Dharma" meaning truth.
86. A Sri Lankan Worker's Mass in *From Shore to Shore*, 17.

"If there is among you anyone in need. . .do not be hard-hearted or tight-fisted toward your needy neighbor."[87]

"When you reap the harvest of your land, you shall not reap to the very edges of your field, or gather the gleanings of your harvest. . .you shall leave them for the poor and the alien: I am the Lord your God."[88]

"You shall not cheat in measuring length, weight, or quantity. . .You shall have honest balances, honest weights. . .I am the Lord your God, who brought you out of the land of Egypt."[89]

"Give justice to the weak and the orphan; maintain the right of the lowly and the destitute."[90]

"But I say to you. . .Love your enemies, do good to those who hate you, bless those who curse you, pray for those who abuse you."[91]

87. Deuteronomy 15:7, NRSV.
88. Leviticus 19:9–10. NRSV.
89. Leviticus 19:35–36, NRSV.
90. Psalm 82:3, NRSV.
91. Luke 6:27, NRSV.

"Do not repay anyone evil for evil. . .Do not be overcome by evil, but overcome evil with good."[92]

"So then, whenever we have an opportunity, let us work for the good of all, and especially for those of the family of faith."[93]

92. Romans 12:17, 21, NRSV
93. Galatians 6:10, NRSV.

42
The Ten Commandments

"I am the Lord your God, who brought you out of the land of Egypt, out of the house of slavery, you shall have no other gods before me. You shall not make an idol. . .You shall not bow down to them or worship them; for I the Lord your God am a jealous God. . .You shall not make wrongful use of the name of the Lord your God, for the Lord will not acquit anyone who misuses his name.

Remember the sabbath day, and keep it holy. Six days you shall labor and do all your work. But the seventh day is a sabbath to the Lord your God; you shall not do any work—you, your son or your daughter, your male or female slave, your livestock, or the resident alien in your towns. . .

Honor your father and your mother, so that your days may be long in the land that the Lord your God is giving you.

You shall not murder.

You shall not commit adultery.

You shall not steal.

You shall not bear false witness against your neighbor.

You shall not covet your neighbor's house, you shall not covet your neighbor's wife, or male or female slave, or ox, or donkey, or anything that belongs to your neighbor."[94]

94. Exodus 20:4–17, NRSV.

43

"Truly, the Eucharistic Liturgy is the climax of the Church's life, the event in which the people of God are celebrating the incarnation, the death, and resurrection of Jesus Christ. . .the Liturgy is not self-centred service and action, but. . .for the building of the one Body of Christ within the economy of salvation which is for all people of all ages. . .Renewed by the Holy Communion and the Holy Spirit the members of the Church are sent to be authentic testimony to Jesus Christ in the world."[95]

"Missionary activity is nothing else, and nothing less, than the manifestation of God's plan, its epiphany and realization in the world. . .by which God. . .clearly brings to its conclusion the history of salvation."[96]

"We affirm that Christ sends his redeemed people into the world as the Father sent him. . .In the church's mission of sacrificial service evangelism is primary."[97]

"Although reconciliation with man [woman] is not reconciliation with God, nor is social action evangelism, nor is political liberation salvation, nevertheless we affirm that evangelism and socio-political involvement are both part of our Christian duty."[98]

95. "The Liturgy after the Liturgy" (1978), in *The Ecumenical Movement*, 365.

96. "Ad Gentes Divinitus" (1965), in *The Basic Sixteen Documents, Vatican Council II*, 453.

97. "The Lausanne Covenant" (1974), in *Making Christ Known*, 28.

98. "The Grand Rapids Report on Evangelism and Social Responsibility"

"Creation is a gift; women and men are to be faithful stewards in caring for the earth. . .The Church has affirmed that the misuse of the world's resources or appropriation of them by a minority. . .betrays the gift of creation since 'whatever belongs to God belongs to all.'"[99]

"In Jesus of Nazareth the Word became a human being. The wonder of his ministry of love persuades Christians to testify to people of every religious and non-religious persuasion of this decisive presence of God in Christ. In him is our salvation."[100]

(1982) in *Making Christ Known*, 178.

99. "Economic Justice for All" (1986), in *Catholic Social Thought*, 586.

100. "Mission and Evangelism—An Ecumenical Affirmation," (1982), in *The Ecumenical Movement*, 382.

44
The Missional Task of the Church

Impacted by the restoring love of Christ, through the Holy Spirit, Christians seek to live as faithful participants in the kingdom of God by being a witness and servant to all with whom they come into contact. And as members of their respective faith communities, they seek to participate in the church's work in the world.

The missional task of the church has its source in God's renewing action in the church and comes to expression in a myriad of ways as the church seeks to be a priestly and prophetic community in the world.

The faith-community is called to proclaim Christ as saviour and lord. Its task is to be good news, bring good news, and to do all it can to be a blessing in all the domains of life. This means that Christians involved in their vocations in society and as present to their neighbours, are to be as salt, light, leaven, and healing oil to all, but especially to the marginalised in society.

There is no domain of life that does not need God's renewing work. Therefore, all in the community of faith are called to be a prayerful and serving presence in all areas of life. Neither politics, economics, or the arts are to be excluded from God's renewing work.

While Christians are called to be witnesses to the good news in Christ, they are also called to be good citizens in society. This does not mean that they necessarily agree with the dominant values of a society, but it does mean that they seek to be God's healing and prophetic good in the world, and that they work for reconciliation and peacemaking.

Christians celebrate God as Creator and Redeemer. This means that they are committed to earth-keeping and nurturing stewardship, as well as seeing people embrace the ethics of the Sermon on the Mount through seeking to live in the way of Jesus.

The task of the church is not to gain social and political power, but to live the gospel and be an incarnational presence in society. Importantly, the faith-community is to be an anticipatory community of God's final future where peace and righteousness will fully reign.

What a challenge! And how much we will need faith, hope, and love and the empowering Spirit to live such and life.

45

"Christ, as light

illumine and guide me.

Christ, as a shield

overshadow me.

Christ under me;

Christ over me;

Christ beside me

on my left and my right.

This day be within and without me,

lowly and meek, yet all-powerful.

Be in the heart of each to whom I speak;

in the mouth of each who speaks unto me.

This day be within and without me,

lowly and meek, yet all-powerful.

Christ as a light;

Christ as a shield;

Christ beside me

on my left and my right."[101]

101. *Celtic Daily Prayer: Book Two*, 867.

46
A People of Prayer

"Almighty God, Father of all mercies,

we your unworthy servants

give you most humble and hearty thanks

for all your goodness and loving-kindness.

We bless you for your creation, preservation, and all the blessings

of this life.

But above all for your immeasurable love

in the redemption of the world by our Lord Jesus Christ,

for the means of grace, and for the hope of glory.

And give us, we pray, such a sense of all your mercies

that our hearts

may be unfeignedly thankful,

that we may show forth your praise,

not only with our lips but with our lives,

by giving up ourselves to your service,

and by walking before you in holiness and righteousness,

all our days.

Through Jesus Christ our Lord,

to whom with you and the Holy Spirit

be honour and glory, for ever and ever. Amen."[102]

102. *Celebrating Common Prayer,* 247.

47

"Hands of Christ

Divine hands of a carpenter. . .

I do not imagine those hands

Forging spears, crafting swords,

Nor designing a new model of bomber;

Those hands, Christ's hands,

Were the hands of a carpenter.

Among feverish hands

That make boats and bombers,

His hands are not found!

His hands bear nail marks,

Heroic signs of sacrifice;

Those hands, bloody hands,

Strong, sinewy, hands of iron,

The sturdy hands of a carpenter

Who quietly shapes life."[103]

103. Francisco E. Estrello quoted in Samuel Escobar, *In Search of Christ in Latin America*, 79.

48
Cry Freedom: Prayers from South America

"O Christ of a continent

whose entrails are red from so much spilt blood.

From diseased ambition,

so many fratricidal swords, so much greed that kills.

Rise up soon

and pronounce your sovereign word

that halts the arrogance

that gallops through these lands.

And usher in for the poor of this [Latin] American land,

a dawning of justice,

a dawning of hope.

And bury forever the night that has been so long. . .

Doesn't it seem, my Christ,

my Lord of hope,

that the hour draws nigh,

that it is already the third morning?

And my America sighs to contemplate you at daybreak."[104]

---

104. Federico Pagura quoted in Samuel Escobar, *In Search of Christ in Latin America*, 304.

49

"For behold, I create new heavens and a new earth, and the former things shall not be remembered. . .I will rejoice in Jerusalem and be glad in my people; no more shall be heard in it the sound of weeping and the cry of distress. . .They shall build houses and inhabit them; they shall plant vineyards and eat their fruit. . .my chosen shall long enjoy the work of their hands."[105]

"He shall judge between many peoples, and shall decide for strong nations afar off; and they shall beat their swords into plowshares, and their spears into pruning hooks; nation shall not lift up sword against nation, neither shall they learn war anymore."[106]

"For I consider that the sufferings of this present time are not worth comparing with the glory that is to be revealed to us. For the creation waits with eager longing for the revealing of the sons of God. . .For we know that the whole creation has been groaning together in the pains of childbirth until now. And not only the creation, but we ourselves, who have the firstfruits of the Spirit, groan inwardly as we wait eagerly for adoption as sons, the redemption of our bodies."[107]

"For the trumpet will sound, and the dead will be raised imperishable, and we shall be changed."[108]

105. Isaiah 65:17–22, ESV.
106. Micah 4:3. ESV.
107. Romans 8:18–23, ESV.
108. 1 Corinthians 15:52, ESV.

"See, the home of God is among mortals. He will dwell with them; they will be his peoples, and God himself will be with them; he will wipe every tear from their eyes. Death will be no more; mourning and crying and pain will be no more, for the first things have passed away."[109]

109. Revelation 21:3–4, NRSV.

50
God's Final Future

The Christian faith has relevance for one's daily life, including family, business, the arts, and politics. But it also has a vision for the life to come in new heavens and a new earth when God will be all in all and God's righteousness and peace will fully flourish.

The Christian church has always confessed the beauty of the life to come, while emphasising the calling we have on this earth to pray for and to seek to do God's good in our world. And the church has resisted the idea that Christians be so heavenly minded as to be no earthly good or to be so involved in daily affairs that God is forgotten and prayer is neglected.

Christians have desired that more of heaven come down to earth; that God's kingdom is more fully amongst us; and that God's future is more fully anticipated in the here and the now.

Throughout the long journey of the Church in history, some Christians have predicted a time of the end of the world, or the thousand-year peaceful reign of Christ in the world, or God's final judgement day. So far, all of these predictions have been wrong.

The waiting time continues. And Christians continue to live in the hope of a final resurrection and new heavens and a new earth in God's kingdom.

It is a challenge to wait. But it is also a blessing. Living in the expectation of God's final future means that we see all of life as provisional and as anticipatory. Nothing of our own making is marked by finality—neither the way we do church, nor our theologies, nor contemporary ideological movements and political endeavours.

Christians believe that what we accomplish in society is but a small echo of God's desire for humanity. Thus, Christians are also prayerful, watchful, discerning, and seeking to be a prophetic witness and a healing presence.

While the biblical story highlights the power of God's redemptive work in Christ and the future Christification of the world, how this will all unfold and when this will take place, lies in the heart of God.

Thus, God's final future will always be the hope of the church as it lives in faith in the God who is alpha and omega and whose promises are yea and amen in Christ. And as the faith-community waits, it seeks to be birthing community through the Word and the Spirit to bring new life to an often not-so-watching world.

51

"The Lord bless you and keep you:

The Lord make His face to shine upon you,

To shine upon you and be gracious,

And be gracious unto you.

The Lord bless you and keep you:

The Lord make His face to shine upon you,

To shine upon you and be gracious,

And be gracious unto you.

The Lord lift up the light

Of His countenance upon you,

The Lord lift up the light

Of His countenance upon you.

And give you peace. And give you peace. And give you peace.

And give you peace.

Amen. Amen. Amen. Amen."[110]

110. Google.com/search?q=hymn+the+lord+bless+you+keep+you+words

52
Benedictions

"The Lord said to Abram, 'Leave your country, your people and your father's household and go to the land I will show you. I will make you into a great nation and I will bless you; I will make your name great and you will be a blessing. I will bless those who bless you, and whoever curses you I will curse; and all peoples of the earth will be blessed through you.'"[111]

"May God be gracious to us and bless us and make his face shine upon us, that your ways may be known on earth, your salvation among all nations. May the peoples praise you, O God; may all the peoples praise you. May the nations be glad and sing for joy, for you rule the peoples justly and guide the nations of the earth."[112]

"When he had led them out to the vicinity of Bethany, he lifted up his hands and blessed them. While he was blessing them, he left them and was taken up into heaven. Then they worshipped him and returned to Jerusalem with great joy."[113]

"May the grace of the Lord Jesus Christ, and the love of God, and the fellowship of the Holy Spirit be with you all."[114]

111. Genesis 12:1–3, NIV.
112. Psalm 67:1–4, NIV.
113. Luke 24:50–52, NIV.
114. 2 Corinthians 13:14, NIV.

"May the God of peace, who through the blood of the eternal covenant brought back from the dead our Lord Jesus, that great Shepherd of the sheep, equip you with everything good for doing his will, and may he work in us what is pleasing to him, through Jesus Christ, to whom be glory for ever and ever. Amen."[115]

"To him who is able to keep you from falling and to present you before his glorious presence without fault and with great joy—to the only God our Savior be glory, majesty, power, and authority through Jesus Christ our Lord."[116]

115. Hebrews 13:20–21, NIV.
116. Jude 24, NIV.

Index of Terms and Questions

Apostles' Creed: In the 390's CE there was already an awareness of this creed. This creed, along with others, was an attempt to identify core beliefs of the Christians faith. Creeds were used in the faith formation of believers and as setting parameters of orthodoxy. See page 7. *Question:* What are your core beliefs? How do they line with the Apostles' Creed? And have you thought of writing a personal creed to live by?

Baptism: This is one of the foundational sacraments of the church. Baptism signifies identification in the death and resurrection of Christ and is the symbol of new life and participation in the faith-community. Some Christian traditions also speak of a Baptism in the Spirit. See pages 51–54. *Question:* In what ways am I called to live the baptismal charism?

Barmen Declaration: Was the statement of the Confessing Church in Germany that opposed Hitler's attempt at the Nazification of the church. The Declaration called for submission of the Lordship of Christ over all other powers, including the cultural and political. See page 17. *Question:* In what ways am I called to live the Lordship of Christ in my daily life, including in my career?

Beatitudes: These important sayings are at the heart of the teaching of Jesus in the Sermon on the Mount that deal with how Christians should live a life of love, forgiveness, and peace-making. Several church traditions rightly stress that these values are to be lived in the here and now through the enabling Spirit. See page 10. *Question:* This way of living is so different than a life of self-assertion and power over others. How can I grow into becoming a person reflecting the beauty of Christ?

Benediction: This is spiritual blessing which is given in the name of the Father, Son, and Holy Spirit. Such a blessing is called performative language which imparts what it promises. See pages 76–78. *Question:* In what ways can I live more fully under the blessing of God and thus be a blessing for others?

Bible: The Bible or Holy Scripture is held by the church to be the Word of God. It speaks of God's purposes in redeeming humanity. The Old Testament speaks of God's purposes with Israel and is preparation to the New Testament with is message of the life, death, and resurrection of Christ and the beginning of the church. The Bible as a historical, literary, and theological book contains the major themes of creation, fall, redemption, and the final consummation of all things. Christians are called to shape their lives in the light of scripture as it is taught in the faith community. Throughout this brief catechism many scriptures are quoted, and some could be committed to memory. *Question:* In what ways can I become more fully attentive to the Word of God?

Celtic Spirituality: Is a rich tradition in the Christian church that emphasises the Trinity, community, a spirituality of daily life, creation care, and a love of witness and service. The book, *Celtic Daily Prayer,* is one resource. See pages 43–44 and 68. *Question:* What can I learn from this tradition in order to live more fully the presence of God in the ordinariness of daily life?

Christ: The person and work of Christ for the salvation of humanity is the central theme of the biblical story. Jesus the Christ is the Son of God and Son of Man. The church confesses Jesus Christ's incarnation, life, death, resurrection, ascension, and his Lordship in the church and in the life of his followers. See page 14 and throughout the catechism. *Question:* In what ways can I be more fully captivated by Christ and to live my life following his example?

Christian: We can speak of the Christian faith, church, art, university and many other institutional realities. This means that these are shaped by Christian values. A Christian is a person who has a faith commitment to Christ, has embraced Christ's salvation, and seeks to live in the way that Christ lived. *Question:* In what ways can I live the Christian life with greater fidelity?

Commandment: The Bible contains commandments and instructions about what we are to believe and how we need to live. These commandments function within a framework of grace, blessing, and enabling. Thus, we are empowered to respond to God's calling and we respond to God out of gratitude rather than obligation. See page 63. *Question:* God is both Saviour and Lord. We can't have one without the other. So, how can I live God's lordship more fully?

Covenant: God is a covenant-making God. In this, God initiates a relationship in the frame of blessing and obedience, favour and responsibility. In covenant-making God seeks to create a visible faith community. See page 20. *Question:* In what ways can the church be a covenant community?

Church: The church is the organisational shape of the faith-community that gathers for worship, teaching, participating in the sacraments, fellowship, and witness and service in society. Pages 20, 39, 66 deal particularly with the church, but there are many references to the church throughout this catechism. *Question:* In what ways can I contribute to the church becoming a more faithful reflection of Christ?

Eschatology: Is the theological term that is used to refer to God's final future when death and suffering will be no more, God's loving rule will be fully manifest, and there will be new heavens and a new earth. Page 74 deals with this topic. *Question:* How can I live more fully today in anticipating God's final future?

Eucharist: This special "meal" instituted by Christ is also called the Lord's Supper or Holy Communion. This is celebrated within the faith-community. And the church believes that in the eucharistic celebration the blessing of Christ's suffering and death is not only remembered, but Christ is present to bless and empower through the Holy Spirit. Pages 55–58 deal with this topic. *Question:* Blessed by the enriching presence of Christ in the eucharist, how can I become bread and drink to others?

Faith: One of the central themes in becoming a Christian and living the Christian life is the theme of faith. Faith is a gift inspired by the Spirit and is a gift we use in believing and trusting God's salvation in Christ and the promises of God in the biblical narratives. This theme occurs throughout the catechism. *Question:* I am saved by faith in what Christ has accomplished on the cross. How can I live that faith in more practical ways?

Father: The scriptures use many terms to describe God, but the most intimate is Father. This is term that Jesus repeatedly used. *Question:* In what ways do I need to grow in seeing God in more personal and intimate ways, rather than in more abstract and distant ways?

Freedom: The heart of the biblical story is that God's salvation brings freedom for individuals and society. This freedom for all, is a freedom of justice, peace, and well-being. Page 46 touches on this. *Question:* How can I pray and work towards a world of freedom where oppression is replaced by care and human flourishing?

Formation: A Christian's calling is to grow into Christlikeness and spiritual maturity. This includes growing in understanding scripture and the faith-tradition of the church. The dimensions of formation include: head (growing in knowing scripture and theology), heart (growing in spiritual practices), and hand (growing in practical areas of witness and service). Page 39 touches on these matters. *Question:* In what ways do I need to place myself open to the ministry of others in my Christian development?

Grace: Living the Christian life is not about self-effort in order to get credit with God. The Christian life is generated and sustained by the grace of God. Grace is God's unmerited beneficence. It is God's smile upon us. *Question:* In what ways can my life be more fully motivated by grace rather than obligation?

Holy Spirit: The church confesses that the Spirit is the third "person" of the Trinity, sent by the Father and the Son to make Christ present to us, to help us understand the scriptures, to work gifts and graces into our lives, and to empower us for service. See pages 48–50. *Question:* Rather than being self-reliant, in what ways can we grow to be more open and reliant on the Spirit graceful work in our lives?

Mission: The God of the Bible is a missional God who constantly reaches out to all that has been created in order to heal, renew, and sustain. As God's people, the church is called to be a witness and servant of the purposes of God in bringing redemption and renewal to our world. See page 66. *Question:* What is God's calling on my life in order to be his witness and servant in our world? And in what ways can I renew and enhance that calling?

Prayer: There are many ways in which we can respond to God, including in worship and service. But prayer is a key way to be in a relationship with God. While we are encouraged to bring all of our concerns to God in prayer, prayer is also about friendship—being held in the heart of God. See pages 1, 2, 36, 49, 69. *Question:* We are often so busy that we neglect prayer. How can we nurture a more prayerful posture in every dimension of our lives?

Prophetic: The church is called to be a healing and peace-making presence in the world. But it is also called to be a discerning community. As such, it is to speak and practice truth and justice to the misuse of power and to champion the cause of the poor and marginalised. See pages 20, 30, 66. *Question:* In what ways can I develop the courage to speak up for those who are wronged?

Redemption: The main mantra of the biblical narratives is the wonder of the God who reaches out to a wounded humanity to bring about restoration and wholeness. The extent of this passion is most clearly seen by God in Christ, taking on humanity in order that we may be restored to the fullness of being made in God's image and likeness. See page 9. *Question:* In what ways can

God's redemptive love more fully penetrate into all the dimensions of my life?

Spiritual Practices: Christian spirituality springs from God's restoration in our lives. In living out this restoration we are called to be people of worship and thanksgiving, attentive listeners to scripture, persons of prayer and contemplative practices, and persons open to advice and correction. These themes are throughout the catechism, but see page 33. *Question:* In what ways can we grow to drink more regularly at the wellsprings that will nurture and deepen our faith?

Trinity: The Christian church confesses that there in one God, Father, Son, and Holy Spirit. This community of God is marked by the most profound love and mutuality. Each of the "persons" of the Trinity is involved in each other's ministry bringing beauty and wholeness. This theme is throughout the catechism. *Question:* In what ways can the doctrine of the Trinity inspire us to live and to work more cooperatively?

Bibliography

Belonging to God: Catechism Resources for Worship. Louisville, KN: Geneva Press, 2003.

Brueggemann, Walter, *The Prophetic Imagination.* Second Edition. Minneapolis, MN: Fortress Press, 2001.

Catechism of the Catholic Church. Manila: ECCCE, 1994.

Catholic Social Thought: The Documentary History. Eds. David J. O'Brien and Thomas A. Shannon. Maryknoll, NY: Orbis Books, 2005.

Celebrating Common Prayer: A Version of the Daily Office SSF. New York: Mowbray, 1994.

Celtic Daily Prayer: Book Two: Farther Up and Farther In. London: William Collins, 2015.

Common Worship: Services and Prayers for the Church of England. London: Church House Publishing, 2000.

Creeds of the Churches: A Reader in Christian Doctrine from the Bible to the Present. Ed. John H. Leith. Garden City, NY: Anchor Books, 1963.

Cunningham, Lawrence S. and Keith J. Egan, *Christian Spirituality: Themes from the Tradition.* New York: Paulist Press, 1996.

Early Anabaptist Spirituality: Selected Writings. The Classics of Western Spirituality. Ed. Daniel Liechty. New York: Paulist Press, 1994.

Escobar, Samuel, *In Search of Christ in Latin America: From Colonial Image to Liberating Savior.* Carlisle, UK: Langham Global, 2019.

Francis and Clare: The Complete Works. The Classics of Western Spirituality. Eds. Regis J. Armstrong & Ignatius C. Brady. New York: Paulist Press, 1982.

Hippolytus, *On the Apostolic Tradition.* Popular Patristic Series. Introduction and Commentary by Alistair Stewart. Crestwood, NY: St Vladimir's Seminary Press, 2001.

Making Christ Known: Historic Mission Documents from the Lausanne Movement, 1974–1989. Ed. John Stott. Grand Rapids, MI: Eerdmans, 1997.

Mysterium Liberationis: Fundamental Concepts of Liberation Theology. Eds. Ignacio Ellacuria and Jon Sobrino. Maryknoll, NY: Orbis Books, 1993.

Of Martyrs, Monks, and Mystics: A Yearly Meditational Reader of Ancient Spiritual Wisdom. Eds. Charles Ringma & Irene Alexander. Eugene, OR: Cascade, 2015.

Psalter Hymnal: Doctrinal Standards and Liturgy of the Christian Reformed Church. Centennial Edition. Grand Rapids, MI: Publication Committee of the Christian Reformed Church, 1959.

Schmemann, Alexander, *For the Life of the World: Sacraments and Orthodoxy.* Crestwood, NY: St Vladimir's Seminary Press, 1973.

The Australian Hymn Book: With Catholic Supplement. Sydney, NSW: Collins, 2001.

The Book of Alternative Services of The Anglican Church if Canada. Toronto: Anglican Book Centre, 1985.

The Doubleday Prayer Collection. Selected and arranged by Mary Batchelor. New York: Doubleday, 1997.

The Ecumenical Movement: An Anthology of Key Texts and Voices. Eds. Michael Kinnamon and Brian E. Cope. Geneva: WCC Publications, 1997.

Vatican Council II. The Basic Sixteen Documents. Ed. Austin Flannery. Northport, NY: Costello Publishing, 1996.

von Balthasar, Hans Urs. *Credo: Meditations on the Apostle's Creed.* Edinburgh: T&T Clark, 1990.

Wyles, Kate, *From Shore to Shore: Liturgies, Litanies and Prayers from Around the World.* London: SPCK, 2003.

www.ingramcontent.com/pod-product-compliance
Lightning Source LLC
Chambersburg PA
CBHW052157090426
42741CB00010B/2309

9 7 9 8 3 8 5 2 0 1 8 7 7